FLY BACK TO THE BRAC, BRIAN BROWN BOOBY

Fly Back to the Brac, Brian Brown Booby
by Elaine A. Powers
Copyright 2017 by Elaine A. Powers
All rights reserved.

ISBN-13: 978-1546330493
ISBN-10: 1546330496
Published by Lyric Power Publishing LLC, Tucson AZ 2015

All information provided is believed and intended to be reliable, but accuracy cannot be guaranteed by the author or the publisher.

FLY BACK TO THE BRAC, BRIAN BROWN BOOBY

BY

ELAINE A. POWERS

ILLUSTRATED BY

SIMONE SCOTT

This book is dedicated to the brown boobies
and the caring Caymanians.

CHAPTER 1. BRIAN ON THE BEACH

Some birds soar as soon as they leave the nest, but not brown boobies. They have to practice flying first, strengthening their wings by flapping, taking short flights that are mostly hopping. Brian Brown Booby had been flapping his wings for days, hoping that today was the day he would fly off the beach and out over the ocean. A strong wind blew onshore from a storm building over the Caribbean Sea. Brian thought it might provide the uplift he needed to get off the ground. However, he wasn't having any luck.

He looked longingly at the fledglings up on the bluff of Cayman Brac. Most booby parents built their nests on top of the bluff that ran through the middle of the island. But Brian's parents had selected a place on the beach. A few other nests were also on the beach, but they were spaced far apart. Brian looked down the shore.

At the nearest nests, other fledglings were strengthening their wings but no one was flying. He looked back at the bluff in time to see a bluff fledging launch out into the air. It rode the wind along edge, soaring briefly before landing again on top.

"That's what I want to do," said Brian. "I wish I had hatched in a bluff nest." Brian looked up and down the beach. "What I need is a high spot. A place where the wind can lift me up. There! That sand dune that's built up along the rock outcropping. That's the highest point around. I wonder if it's high enough to launch myself. Maybe I don't need a bluff. Beach boobies can soar as well, no, better than bluff boobies."

Even though he flapped his wings, Brian had to hop over the beach and up to the top of the sand dune. Once there, he flapped again in excitement. The wind ruffled his feathers. He hopped up, extending his wings as far as they could go. "Today I fly," said Brian to the wind. Brian positioned himself, ready to fly. The wind pushed on his feathers. He hopped up as far as he could. The wind rushed under his wings and lifted him up. "I'm flying," Brian cried. He flapped his wings. "I'm flying."

The wind took Brian out over the water. "I'm soaring," he yelled. The wind carried him over the channel beside the beach and over the sand bar where big waves crashed.

But Brian soon realized he wasn't flying. The wind was blowing him offshore. He flapped his wings, but they did nothing. As the wind died down, he lost altitude and was headed for a crash landing in the water.

"I can swim," said Brian as he got closer to the crashing waves. "But there might be sharks in the water. I might not be able to get away."

CHAPTER 2. SAFE LANDING

Brian was tired of flapping and still falling. All around him was the vast ocean. Brian didn't want to land on the water. "I have to try to make it back to the beach." His wings flapped slower and slower. He looked all around him, looking for something other than the water to land on. There it was! A landing place. The boat was slowly cruising along the channel. Brian aimed toward the boat. He folded his wings to go as fast as he could. The boat approached slowly. Brian lost altitude…then the boat was underneath him. Plop! Brian landed on the deck of the boat.

The people on the boat were quite surprised. A young boy ran over to Brian.

"Wow, birds are falling from the sky," a woman observed.

"Hey, Captain, we've got another passenger."

"I see that," came the reply.

"What an interesting looking bird," a man said.

Brian flapped his wings.

"Wow, look at that wingspan. It must be at least four feet," said a woman.

"Can he stay?" asked the young boy, looking pleadingly at his father, the captain.

"As long as he doesn't eat any of the fish we caught."

"He can have my fish," said the boy. He reached slowly towards the bird, but Brian hopped backward away from the approaching hand.

"I don't think he wants you to pet him, son," said the captain.

"That's okay, we can just talk," said the boy kneeling down beside Brian. "Hi, bird, my name is Charley. What kind of bird are you?"

"He's a brown booby, son" said the captain. The other people on the boat huddled around the bird. Several took out their cameras or cell phones to take photos.

"What a funny name. Booby, booby," said Charley.

"Some people say its slang for stupid," replied the captain.

"Why?" asked Charley.

"They liked to land on sailing ships where the sailors would catch and eat them."

"People ate them because they were friendly?" the woman asked.

"Afraid so, ma'am," was the reply.

Charley sat down next to Brian. "Don't worry, brown booby, I won't let anyone eat you."

"I thought boobies were dark brown with a white chest," commented the woman.

"This is a juvenile. You can tell by the gray-brown coloration," said the captain.

Charley grabbed Brian's long tail. Brian turned in surprise.

"Be careful, son, boobies have very sharp bills. You don't want to be bitten."

"I'm sorry, booby, I didn't mean to scare you. You don't need to be afraid of me."

"How long until we reach Grand Cayman, Captain?" asked the woman.

"About six hours. The storm is going to slow our progress," the captain replied.

"Well, at least we have some entertainment. So, tell us about yourself, booby," the man said. "I'm going to throw out a fishing line. Maybe I can catch us some fish, booby."

The boat accelerated towards its destination, Grand Cayman. Brian realized the boat was going away from his home on the Brac. He flapped his wings, willing himself to fly back but he was still too weak. He cuddled close to the boy. He was afraid. Charley cuddled him, gently petting his feathers.

Charley moved to the railing to look out over the ocean. Brian hopped up onto the seat, then the bow to join him. Brian positioned himself on the railing.

"It's beautiful out there, isn't it booby?" said Charley. "You're so lucky you get to live there and eat fish. I love eating fish."

"We're almost home, booby. You can stay with me in my bedroom," said Charley pointing at the land coming into sight, the island of Grand Cayman.

"This is wrong," thought Brian. "I must fly home, back to the Brac."

Brian flapped his wings, then lessened his body weight by pooping. His parents kept him well-fed, so he had a sizable amount to unload.

"Oh, what is that awful smell?' asked the captain.

"Booby pooped," responded Charley.

"Get that stinking bird off my teak deck. Get him off my boat!" commanded the captain.

"But I want to keep him," cried Charley.

"Off," said the captain, picking up Brian and throwing him overboard. Brian hit the water with a splash, but quickly righted himself.

"Bye bye, booby, I'll miss you," yelled Charley, waving at the bird bobbing in the ship's wake.

CHAPTER 3. ARRIVAL ON SEVEN MILE BEACH

Brian bobbed in the waves. He was confused as he watched the boat disappear into the distance. He paddled in a circle, searching the horizon, searching for land. He paddled in bigger circles, going a little farther each time. He flapped his wings, desperate to fly. But no matter how hard he flapped, he plopped back down into the waves. He flapped one last time with his remaining strength and propelled himself forward through the water.

"There! There in the distance is land," he exclaimed. He paddled rapidly. "I can see a beach! Maybe it's the beach where I was born."

He paddled and paddled until he felt sand under his feet. Despite the waves pushing and knocking him over, he waddled ashore — his webbed feet were much better for swimming than walking. He gratefully sat down on the warm sand.

He looked down the beach. No boobies. He looked the other way down the beach. No boobies that way either. But there were many, many people. He knew people from the Brac but not this many.

These people scurried over the beach like crabs. Brian was scared and felt very, very alone.

"I want to go home," he said, only to himself.

Determined, he tried to flap. Brian knew which way it was to get back to the Brac but his wings were too weak. "Maybe I could swim," he thought. "No, it's too far and too dangerous. I'll stay here. Maybe there are other boobies. I just need to look."

He flapped and hopped along the beach but there were only people, everywhere. "I'll rest for a while and then go looking for other boobies," thought Brian. "I'm hungry, I'm thirsty and I'm very, very tired."

He sat down on the beach, looking towards home, heedless of the people swarming the beach around him.

CHAPTER 4. BRIAN IS FOUND ON THE BEACH

Brian was sitting on the beach, wishing it was the Brac, still too tired to move. A person approached him and looked at him. Brian opened his eye and looked at the man, leaning over him. Too tired to be afraid, Brian closed his eyes.

"My heavens, it's a brown booby," the man said. "You don't belong on this island. Brown boobies are only found on the Sister Islands. How did you get here? It's too far for even an adult brown booby to fly. You need help, friend. Let me take you to the wildlife rescue. Don't be afraid, I'm going to wrap you in this towel to protect both of us. If you promise not to bite me, I won't hold your bill closed."

The man gently wrapped Brian in the towel. Brian was too tired to bite so he kept still and let the man lift him. The man carried Brian across the beach to his car in the parking lot, placed him in the back seat of the car, and buckled him in with the seat belt. "Safety first," said the man.

When the man drove up to the animal hospital, several people came out to the car, picked Brian up and rushed him into the exam room. Brian was glad of the towel when they placed him on the cold metal table.

"I prefer it to be warm like outside," he squawked. The vet gently examined him. The aide was less gentle, poking Brian to remove some of his blood.

Brian was given a thorough examination, maybe too thorough in his opinion. The vet felt up and down his body, carefully extending each wing and leg. He was placed on his back and his wings extended. The vet was very gentle. Brian was taped to a board and put in an x-ray machine.

"I don't like this," thought Brian.

"We can check to see if any of your bones are broken or if you've swallowed any fishing hooks. Wouldn't want you to have any hooks inside you," said the vet to Brian. "Good news, booby. I don't see any breaks or foreign objects like hooks."

The vet gave Brian some fluids because he was dehydrated. Brian drank some of the electrolyte solution while the vet inserted a needle under his skin to give him saline, too.

"And I'm going to give you some anti-inflammatories to stop any infections you might have. With some care, you should be good as new."

"I am feeling better," thought Brian as the fluids rehydrated him.

The vet told the man from the beach about Brian's condition. "The booby is badly dehydrated and severely exhausted. But the good news is that no bones are broken nor are there internal injuries. He needs time and food."

"Should I call around to see if any foster homes are available," asked the vet's assistant.

"No," the vet replied. "All Brac animals have to be returned to the Brac for rehabilitation. And as soon as possible. Call the rescuer there and tell her a brown booby is coming her way."

"You know, if we keep the booby, we could use him as a mascot for fundraising. Or how about we take the booby back down to the beach and let everyone see him fly off toward his home on the Brac? I'm sure the local TV and newspapers would cover it. We might even make it onto international news."

"No, wild animals belong back in the wild. The booby can't fly the 80 miles to Brac, even if he was healthy. The responsible thing to do is get him back home. I suspect people brought him to Grand Cayman and now people are going to help him fly back to Cayman Brac."

Brian relaxed in his warm crate. He felt better already and if anyone had asked him, he would have told them "I want to go home."

CHAPTER 5. BRIAN FLIES HOME

The local news had covered his arrival and now they were delighted to report that Brian would be returning home. During his stay on Grand Cayman, he had been named Brian, the Brac Brown Booby.

"Brian flew back to the Brac earlier this afternoon," the news proclaimed. "But he didn't fly using his own wings but the airplane wings of the country's airline. They were proud to help return this Bracker home."

While all the other passengers climbed out of the airplane, Brian waited patiently. All the people got off. Finally, it was Brian's turn. The pet carrier he was in was gently lifted and carried out into the terminal. The rescuer was waiting. She would take him and make sure he was healthy and released back to his family.

Since Brian had received medical attention on Grand Cayman, the rescuer took Brian down to the beach area where other brown boobies congregated.

She carefully removed him from the carrier and placed him on the beach. The other boobies watched intently but from a safe distance.

"I don't know if this your home beach, but hopefully, it is close enough," she said to Brian as she placed him on the sand. The rescuer left the beach but watched to see what would happen. Brian flapped his wings but didn't fly. He settled down on his spot on the beach. The rescuer waited to see if the other boobies would welcome the newcomer but none of the other birds approached Brian. "Maybe they just need some time," the rescuer said, as she left the beach, hopeful for Brian's future.

The other boobies waited until the rescuer was out of sight. An adult booby hopped toward Brian with her head and neck stretched forward. Brian was still tired and sat motionless. The adult honked at Brian and made an exaggerated bow.

Brian rose to his feet, concerned by the adult's aggressive behavior. But Brian wasn't fast enough. The adult jabbed at Brian with her bill and a downward thrust of her wings. "Ouch," cried Brian. "Please don't bite me."

Now scared, Brian hopped away from the adult. Another fledgling behind him jabbed at him, too. "Get away from me. Leave me alone," Brian pleaded.

Brian hopped forward toward the waves lapping on the beach, trying to escape the hostile boobies. Another adult booby joined in the chase. They didn't stop jabbing at him until Brian had hopped on some rocks at the shoreline.

The waves splashed him. He was cold, hungry and now frightened of the other boobies.

CHAPTER 6. BRIAN CAN'T GO HOME AGAIN

When the rescuer checked on Brian the next day, she found him sitting alone off to the side of the beach from where she had left him. "Did the other boobies force you off their beach? Are the other boobies shunning you?" she asked as she saw the rest of the boobies keeping their distance.

"Maybe leaving you in the crowd was the wrong idea. I don't know where your nest is. I'm sorry if I put you in other boobies' territory," she said to Brian. "I'll take you down the shore to a more secluded area." She wrapped Brian in a towel and gently carried him over the rocks to a stretch of beach that didn't have any boobies.

"This is the perfect place," gently setting him on the sand well above the high tide line. "Get a good night's sleep, Brian. I'll be back to check on you in the morning. Feel free to fly off with the dawn."

The next morning, the rescuer returned to the secluded beach. There sat Brian, right where she had left him.

"You look too forlorn and helpless. You aren't getting your own food and your parents aren't around to feed you. I have to take you back to my home."

The rescuer gently picked up Brian, set him back into the pet carrier and placed him in her car. Brian sat quietly. It was cozy in the towel in the carrier.

Once she reached her home, she took Brian out and placed him on her sand yard by the ocean.

"Maybe you'll feel more willing to fly without all the other boobies bothering you, Brian. There's the ocean. You are free to fly away whenever you want. In case you want to stay overnight, I'll get you some fish to eat."

The rescuer went to the local grocery stores. "Would you have some small fish that I could have to feed Brian the Brown Booby?"

"Of course," was the reply. "Have some ballyhoo. I'm sure the booby will enjoy it."

Brian did enjoy the ballyhoo. The rescuer held the food out to Brian. He took the fish in his bill. Then he flipped it and flipped it until it was in the proper position for swallowing, head first. The fish quickly slid down his throat. He looked at the rescuer as if she was his parent. He signaled that he wanted more fish but the rescuer didn't offer him more.

"Goodnight, Brian. Fly off with the sunrise," said the rescuer. Brian sat down, tired but a little less hungry. For the first time in a long time, he felt safe.

Despite the rescuer's hope, Brian was still there in the morning. As the rescuer approached Brian, he flapped his wings and hopped a few steps away.

"You can't fly!" exclaimed the rescuer. Tears collected in her eyes. "How will you join the other brown boobies if you can't fly?"

The rescuer retrieved another ballyhoo. "Maybe you need another day to gain your strength." Brian eagerly ate the offered fish. He flapped his wings a few times. "Tomorrow," the rescuer said. "Tomorrow you will fly. You rest today."

However, the next day came and Brian still sat on the rescuer's beach. "What will become of you if you can't fly, Brian?" the rescuer asked. "Could you fly before you got to Grand Cayman? Have you lost your ability to fly? How will you get it back?" I wish you could tell me what was wrong," she said as she fed Brian his daily ballyhoo. "Or are you just too young and you don't know how to fly yet?"

Each day, the rescuer grew sadder. Tears rolled down her face as she watched the other brown boobies flying by, flying high in a line into the sky. People on Brac were very supportive of her efforts to help Brian, providing the fish for his meals. Feeling better now that he was fed, Brian would flap his wings but he struggled to take off.

"I must fly," he said to himself, since the other boobies were off into the distance.

"Flap harder," the rescuer would say, encouraging him. "Keep flapping, you can do it." She even flapped her arms to show him what to do.

Days passed. Brian flapped and hopped but he didn't fly. "I may not be able to fly but I do like the fish the person gives me. But it's not right to be fed by a person. I want to feed myself. To dive into the water and catch a fish," he thought to himself.

CHAPTER 7. MAYBE TODAY

Each morning, the rescuer found Brian still sitting on her beach. Together they would watch the lines of other boobies fly by.

"Go with them, Brian, please go with them," the rescuer would say. She cried but she wouldn't let the young bird see. She looked at him closely. "Is there something wrong with your wings? Are you injured? Maybe your muscle is damaged. That wouldn't be seen on an X-ray. I wish you could tell me why you aren't flying," said the rescuer.

"I enjoy having you here," said the rescuer, "but you need to join your own kind. I can't be your flock."

The rescuer reported Brian's lack of progress to the vet on Grand Cayman. "Let's hope he needs a little more time to get stronger. Keep feeding him." The vet's supportive words did not ease the rescuer's concerns.

She researched booby development in books. She went to the beach with the booby nests and watched the other young boobies.

"I'm trying to be positive, but it's breaking my heart to find you still here on my beach gazing out over the ocean," she said to Brian. The flock of boobies, both adult and juveniles like Brian, still flew by each morning on their way out to the sea to feed.

"Come on, Brian. Come fly with us," they would call.

"I'm coming," Brian would reply, but every morning he would fail to fly. Then he would sit quietly in the yard.

"He looks so sad," the rescuer would tell everyone.

One morning was different. "Brian, bad news. I need to get you more fish. Your meal will be late," said the rescuer as she came out the door to the beach. "Nobody has any fish, so we're waiting for a delivery."

"Hey, Brian, come along with us. We're headed out to sea to feed," said the brown boobies on their morning flight along the beach.

"I'm going to feed right here," declared one of the flying boobies. She folded her wings and plunged rapidly into the water. The booby surfaced with fish in her bill. A skillful flip of the fish and the fish slid down her throat. "Delicious." The boobies continued on their way out to sea.

But Brian wasn't listening. Brian was flapping his wings. "I'm hungry and I'm going to catch my own food. No more being fed by people."

He turned his body in the direction of the departing boobies. He was flapping his wings harder than he ever had before. He hopped up onto the tallest rock and flapped. His feet lifted off the rock.

But this time he didn't hop, he FLEW! His body rose into the air.

"Go, Brian, go," the rescuer yelled. "Keep flying."

Brian did keep flying. He flew over the beach. He flew over the waves breaking on the shore. He flew over the ocean. He flew to catch up with the flock of brown boobies. He flew off with them.

People throughout the Cayman Islands celebrated: "The brown booby Brian is flying!"

Every morning, the rescuer would watch the flock of brown boobies flying by her beach, knowing that Brian was among them.

"Keep flying, Brian!"

AFTERWORD

The story of Brian the Brown Booby (*Sula leucogaster*) from Cayman Brac is a true story. The only part of the story that is unknown is how Brian got to Grand Cayman, 80 miles from his home on Cayman Brac. When it was determined that he was too young to fly, the rescuers concluded that someone took him there and abandoned him on the beach.

Many volunteers and organizations worked together to rehabilitate Brian and ensure his return to his proper place in the skies and ocean around Cayman Brac.

ACKNOWLEGMENTS

I thank Bonnie Scott Edwards for telling me about Brian and encouraging me to write his story. I greatly appreciate Simone Scott for creating colorful illustrations that evoke the spirit of the islands so well. Thanks to Pamela Bickell, Brad Peterson, and Kate J. Steele for their critical reading and insights. I am grateful for my editor, Nora Miller, without whom this book would not be possible.

I also thank the Brackers, who always welcome me to their island of Cayman Brac.

THE AUTHOR

Elaine A. Powers, originally from Peoria, IL, currently resides in Tucson, AZ. After a career as a laboratory biologist, she is now pursuing her dream of writing science-based children's books and murder mysteries as well as continuing her work as a citizen scientist for iguana conservation. Elaine has taken part in iguana surveys in the Bahamas and the Cayman Islands.

She authored booklets to help people tell the difference between the invasive green iguana and the native iguanas. She has been working with several reptile conservation groups, including the International Reptile Conservation Foundation.

Elaine first visited Cayman Brac to work with the Sister Island Rock Iguanas. The island has inspired her to return time and time again and write more stories.

For more information, visit her website www.elaineapowers.

THE ILLUSTRATOR

Simone Scott knew she wanted to go to Art College before she finished high school. At Dive and Photo, Tiara learned about photography and slide processing allowing her to make a slide portfolio of paintings. Her portfolio earned her a full CI Government Scholarship to Ringling School of Art and Design. She returned to the Brac in 1994 and opened a small gallery, Simone's YFE Art Gallery located in her parents craft shop NIM Things.

In 1998 Simone joined the board of the National Gallery of the Cayman Islands and began working with the National Gallery in 2007. Ms Scott works with the National Gallery as their Cayman Brac and Little Cayman Rep / Instructor and by CTA for Heritage Arts Education as Brac Program Coordinator.

Simone has received numerous awards including the distinguished National Bronze Award for Creativity in the Arts and Chairman's Award from CNCF. While Simone loves to travel, her home Cayman Brac provides lots of inspiration for her paintings, digital art and photography.

www.ingramcontent.com/pod-product-compliance
Lightning Source LLC
Chambersburg PA
CBHW041509280526
45792CB00004B/1197